No Batteries Required

by
Ellen Dooling Reynard

YELLOW ARROW
PUBLISHING
Baltimore, Maryland, USA

No Batteries Required
Copyright © 2021 by Yellow Arrow Publishing
All rights reserved.

Library of Congress Control Number: 2021934221
ISBN (paperback): 978-1-7350230-4-5

Cover art by Alexa Laharty (Instagram @alexaelisabeth).
Interior design by Yellow Arrow Publishing.
For more information, see yellowarrowpublishing.com.

Contents

Acknowledgments   1

moments and non moments

    non moments   7

    Easter 1949   9

    Your Birthday   11

    Din of Deafness   13

    The Longest Night   15

    Questions   17

    Your Hands   19

    NYC   21

    Ashes to Ashes   23

Life's Journey Home

    Fabric of Friendship   27

    Creation   29

    Fredrica   31

    Ladybug   33

    Your Path   35

    Old Age   37

Other Creatures

    Right to Life   41

    Grace   43

    The Black Cat   45

Linking	47
The Cricket	49
By the Lake	51
Montana	53
Walking Sleep	55

Seasoned with Humor

A Riddle	59
When PG&E Cuts Our Power	61
Montana Recipes	63
Zhuzh	65
No Batteries Required	67

About the Author — 69

Acknowledgments

Current Magazine, 2019
"Right to Life"

Inscape Magazine, 2019
"The Cricket" and "Your Hands"

Lighten Up On Line (online), October 2019
"No Batteries Required"

WestWard Quarterly, January 2020
"Easter 1949"

The Writers Club (online), February 2020
"non moments"

Muddy River Poetry Review (online), May 2020
"Montana" and "Old Age"

Silver Pen (online), May 2020
"Creation"

Wax Poetry Poets of the World: 1st Prize, June 2020
"Walking Sleep"

Modern Poetry Quarterly Review (online), October 2020
"Din of Deafness"

~~

My appreciation for the encouragement and editorial advice of Judie Rae, for the input from my poetry writing group, and for the loving support of my children, Fred, Matthew, and Linda.

NO BATTERIES REQUIRED

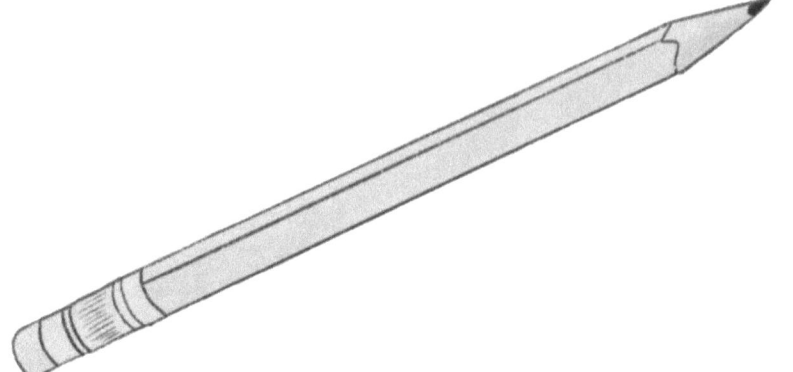

moments and non moments

non moments

roll to a stop behind 20 other cars
waiting for the flagman to let you proceed
lean your head on your hand
fuming about construction zones
power outages doctors' waiting rooms
where overhead clocks tick to show you
your appointment was 15 minutes
25 minutes 40 minutes ago

objecting your life away
dreaming of being somewhere else
mumbling "get on with it"
fidgeting fingers tapping foot

get on with what when you roll to a halt
20 cars between you and the flagman
get on with what when you are thrust
into 48 hours of darkness
when the waiting room clock clicks
to tell you the doctor is one hour late?

get on with life you say but what about
life in all those non moments
does it seep into another reality
freeze like a stored embryo does it die
then come back to life when the flagman
turns his sign from **STOP** to **SLOW**
when the lights come on
when the receptionist calls your name?

get on with life you say
these non moments are a nuisance
we should do away with them you say

then life speaks
what you call non moments
are presents of presence

Easter 1949

Winter didn't give up easily in Western Montana
where the Continental Divide loomed 1,000 feet
above our ranch house. Easter came early that year, the snow
still knee deep even for my father in his boots.

We children spent the night before wondering
whether there would still be an egg hunt in spite of the snow
but when Easter morning dawned, sun-scattered diamond lights
over the white fields, Mother and Daddy told us
the Easter Bunny had just passed by.

We had breakfast, washed dishes, did our chores under Mother's
watchful eye while Daddy went out to pitch hay for the cattle.
After we put on snow pants and ski caps
and mittens and parkas and boots, Mother gave us our baskets
and we scampered out the back door into the shining morning.

Montana winters were every color you ever imagined
and some you hadn't: pink and orange shadows
under purple willows which ran along the banks of blue-iced
ponds, snow sparkled gold silver blue mauve red.

Your breath crackled, tiny icicles lined your nostrils
so you pulled your scarf up to breathe through its itchiness.
The sound of your feet on the snow scritched so loud
it was hard to sneak up on anyone—especially the Easter Bunny.

My brothers and sisters ran whooping across
the front yard and down to the creek;
soon their baskets were filled with many colored eggs.
I was the youngest and my infant independence led me toward
the chicken house instead of following
my siblings' stampede to the barn.

I trod carefully over the snow's crusted surface, etched
with the prints of squirrels and birds—but no Easter Bunny tracks.
Then from the left, a trail of man-sized boot prints barely
broke through the crust. I followed the tracks to the fence,
and there, snuggled against the gate in the sunshine, the most
beautiful gold, red, and yellow Easter egg I had ever seen.
I took off my mitten to pick it up; it was warm in my hand.

I crunched back to the house to show Mother my treasure,
thinking to myself that even the Easter Bunny
had to put on boots and mittens when Easter came
in the middle of winter.

Your Birthday

Like rain on the leaves and roots
of oak trees that drink each drop,
rustle under each shower,
life seeps in, irrigating
your inner landscape with joy,
sorrow, doubt, understanding,
until the sum of moments,
mornings, midnights, months,
add up to another year.

Now your reservoirs are filled,
wavelets licking sandy shores,
yet again you are thirsty
for another year of rain.

Din of Deafness

The empty hallway stretches between them,
filled with echoes. He arches his neck,
creases his brow, as though that will make sense
of the meaningless sounds bouncing from the walls.

She strains to make him understand,
her hopeless cries turn shrill and the hallway
lengthens, resounding with pieces
of syllables, howling vowels.

He shrugs in anger, as if it were her fault
he cannot hear, then retreats into isolation,
she withdraws into her shell. Two
lonely crustaceans divided by silence.

The Longest Night

You called me mon ange gardien,
my special nicknames were always in French.

As I lay beside you on that longest night, and your breath
struggled, unwilling to let you go, my eyes were dry,
while yours watched the moving scene
that only you could see.

I longed to know what you saw but that was
for your eyes alone. I stayed close
with mute attention to listen for the distant
summons so you might better hear its call.

Your last outbreath was long prolonged,
until it was no more. Your eyes dimmed
to this world, and opened
to what only you could see.

I smoothed your hair, and kissed your lips, still warm.
Now you are mon ange gardien.

Questions

Who surfaces in the silence of the mind,
between heartbeats, between each breath?
Who is known, like the smell of new rain,
yet as unknown as the source of the wind?

What is the sudden silence that startles the sleeper?
What happens between the last stroke of midnight
and the first second of the new day? What is the light
seen only from the corner of the eye?

Where does the rainbow begin and where does it end?
Where is the source of the river that leads to the sea?
Where is the cave that holds the secret, known only to the one
who lives there, unknown to idle curiosity?

When will dusk become night and dawn become day?
When is the moment between past and future?
When was morning forgotten in the mad dash
from sunrise to sunset, overlooking the wisdom of noon?

Why does the sleeper awake, then fall again into dreams?
Why is the call to set sail unheard as the ship lies
anchored in still water? Why does the poet ask
unanswerable questions in the search for truth?

Questions that begin with the sound of the wind—*wh*—
resound unknown in the heart. The orphan question
HOW stands alone in the mind, unmoved
by the breeze, in its quest for the already known.

Your Hands

One night when we were young,
we sat on a stone wall listening
to the sea. My palms, my fingers cold
on the stone, the warmth of your arm
so near. Your finger touched mine
and my hand caught fire.

Now, like stained glass windows,
the rooms of my house glow
with the light of your paintings,
your graphite drawings of water,
stone, earth, and air, images of sun
and shadow, legend and creation.

I stroke the paper, the canvas;
I remember how you held
the pencil, the brush.
Your hands, your hands.

NYC

In the surging crowd, you prance your mindless dance
from here to there, hustle, bustle, sidestep, dodge.
What is that beyond, behind?
Deafened by horns and sirens' shrieks,
blinded by **WALK   DON'T WALK** flashing green and red.
What is that, behind, beyond?

Spent, you stop the sidestep, dodge,
uncover your ears to listen, your eyes to look,
beyond the blare, behind the glare:
that echo, like no other sound
that glow, like no other light
that promenade, like no other dance.

Ashes to Ashes

I am with you,
all the while
knowing that only you
can know this exquisite pain.
I am with you because your loss
brings mine back again where I must
step one foot at a time, breathe one breath
at a time, to search for that shaded pathway
I have now to walk alone without the one who
gave me my meaning. At times this is a rocky
road, and other moments, a track climbing up
the foothills, which winds through flowered
slopes to the waterfall. I look backward,
through all my yesteryears, to the day
of loss, and I ask what is still to be
glimpsed, listened to, sensed?
Today I wish that you and I
both might find the way
which lies waiting for
our footfalls to take us home
to ourselves, alone yet not alone.

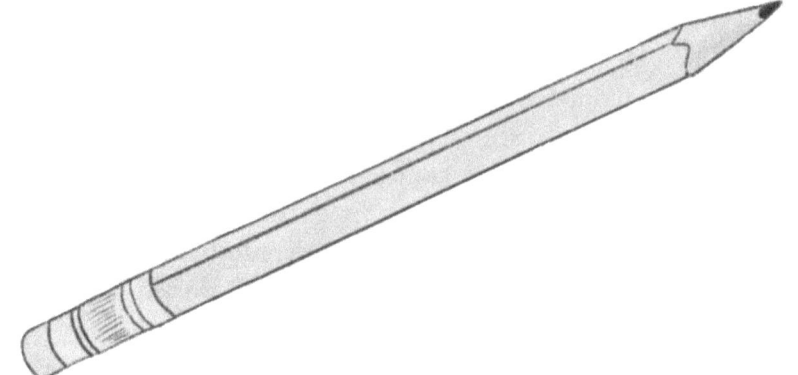

Life's Journey Home

Fabric of Friendship

Many yesterdays ago you and I
were children, we learned how
to escape when grownups got boring,
and to keep the secret when
your father turned 50.

Another yesterday, adolescents
in rebellion against everything,
we walked up the hill, away
from our houses, grumbling
our frustrations about grownups
and their rules.

These bonds of objection,
the fabric of our childhood kinship,
frayed when we became adults,
our parents became our allies,
and we imposed new sets
of rules on our children.

In our middle years we celebrated
joys and suffered sorrows,
the unraveled threads of our childhood
companionship lay like lint on the closet floor.

Now you and I are old, the tapestry
of our lives has been mended and darned
so many times that little of the original
weave remains.

When I see you now, I ask myself
whether our friendship endures,
is the warp and weft still strong
enough to weave new rows?

Creation

suns and moons and stars shone
down on me   my bed was ice mud sand
washed by rain dried by wind
I lay mute and still   I was stone

one day the tempest came
earth air fire water pierced me
through and through
then for timeless time I slept

suns and moons and stars shine
down on me   my bed is ice mud sand
washed by rain dried by wind
I burn I ache I shiver   I am no longer stone.

Fredrica

She was a tiny woman, small-boned,
a bit stooped in her final years.
That was just her body, which caused
her so much pain toward the end.

Inside her little frame, hidden
from a cursory glance,
dwelled a spirit as strong as the eagle,
as steady as the mountain.

In her long life as pupil
of her teachers, comrade
of her fellow students, mentor
to those younger,

she directed our comings and goings
with the expertise of an orchestral conductor:
few words, but those she spoke
cut to the bone.

She left us quietly with no complaint
and stepped into the unknown
with no backward glance,
with no regret.

Now she is mist on the mirror
we hold up to the light;
now she is missed
by those who seek her image there.

Ladybug

When she was four, the child watched
a ladybug walk the length of a blade of grass,
intent on its journey, each step a discovery,
no concern for yesterday or tomorrow.
All that mattered was that endless moment,
one step to the next, to the end
of the grass blade and onto the rose's stem.

When she was 14, the girl began to measure
her yesterdays, plan her tomorrows, and forgot
that once-upon-a-time had no beginning or end.

When she was 34 with a toddler at her knee,
the woman barely noticed, while the child watched
the creature's every move, as a ladybug
climbed between the rose stem's thorns.

When she was 84, the old one dropped
her past like a well-worn sweater and greeted each
new day with surprise. She sat in her rocking chair
as the sun rose from behind the hill, and saw
a ladybug reach the top of the stem
and blend with the red-orange rose petal.

Your Path

You are a teenager, looking for the meaning
of your life. Sometimes you wonder how
it will be when you are old and gray.
Will you still be searching?
Will you find yourself
on the forest trail
that leads up to
the mountains?
You will find
that your meandering
path, beaten by passing feet,
loses itself between the rocks, then
it reappears by the waterfall, footprints
leading up to the summit, where you will look
back to see the whole of your life's long journey home.

Old Age

These are the best years when it is no longer
necessary to prove anything to anyone
when it is safe to let go and enjoy
the free fall from obligation to exploration

as if everything past is yet to be discovered
in memory's watchful reconsideration
as if this moment is yet to be savored when we step
onto the slippery rocks of an unknown passage.

Leave it to the young to ford new crossings climb
higher dive deeper know the unknowable so we
old ones might step out into a new world as immigrants
hungry for opportunity thirsty for life yet to be lived.

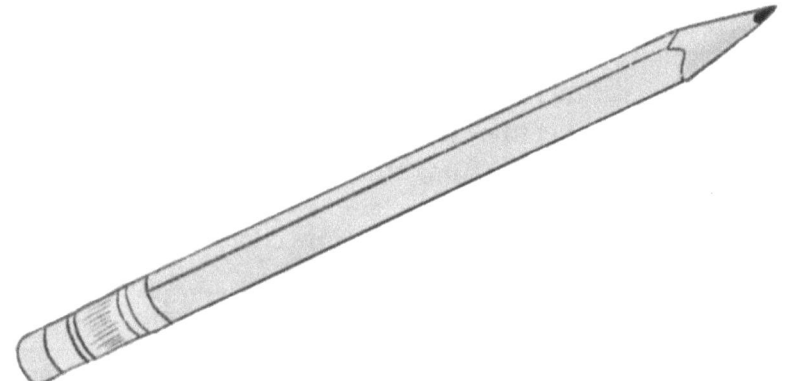

Other Creatures

Right to Life

Rippling black fur, matted with burs,
he ambles along the forest floor
and into the clearing,
where my family is picking bear grass.

My sisters do not see him at first, intent
as they are to find that special white flower
for Saturday's wedding.
But the husbands and brothers,
ever watchful for such an opportunity,
cock their guns and take aim.

"No," I cry, "what's wrong with you?
Why the guns? Why must you kill?"
The creature lumbers into the shadows
and the men lower their rifles.

As rage melts, I put my hand on my belly
and feel the stirring of my unborn child.

Grace

We stop near the forest glade
in the drowsing afternoon
while shadows darken, brushstrokes
of ink over the meadow.

You say you want to see the fawns
come out to play. I tell you, hush,
they hear us, our meaningless words
make shivers ripple over their dusky hides.

As we wait, breath held, the doe
steps alone from the woodland's
edge, and regards us with lucid eyes,
bottomless pools of attentiveness.

For one motionless moment she stands still
as stone, then turns to blend with the trees.
We return to our chatter, deaf to the silence,
blind to the leaf shimmer signs of her passage.

If we were to follow, silent and listening,
eyes open to the unknown trail,
would she simply lead us away from her fawns
or would she also show us a new path home?

The Black Cat

Someone's at the door!
Paws tucked beneath her, she sinks
to the floor, shadowless meld of black,
creeps toward her hiding place
under the blanket under the chair.

Stranger gone danger past, she reemerges,
ears pointed forward, every hair on the alert
to question the safety of her home,
then straightens to tiptoe
one paw in front of the other
on the balance beam she alone can see.

A scrap of crumpled paper beckons,
claws retracted, she nudges it, testing
to see if it's alive. Hearing it rustle, she taps
harder and soon she's running,
the star of a solo game of volleyball,
passing the paper from paw to paw
in perfect coordination.

Goal achieved, she sits down, yawns,
licks her foot six times to wash her face
with drowsy purpose, then hops onto her bed
next to the window, curls three times
around herself and sinks down to sleep.

Linking

On the path beside my house my mind ranges,
a meander of mundane adhesions, not unlike
spider thread linking the propane tank
to an unseen anchor under the eaves of my roof.

Undulating silk, glowing glue dried by the breath
of a breeze, awaits the tightrope walk of its creator.
My wandering wonderings, a slender bridge
between here, and where?

The Cricket

The cricket appears from nowhere
to sit on the rim of my water glass.
After flexing his various legs,
he turns and walks along the rim,
tiny gymnast on a balance beam.

Then he stops,
straightens and rebends his two back legs,
and disappears.

It takes a moment to find him again,
on the hydrangea in a vase six inches away.
In a space of time too short to measure,
he moved from one world to another.

Do I also belong to two worlds?
Are they in fact not so distant,
but as close together as his?
Can he teach me,
in a moment too short to measure,
how to move from one to the other?

By the Lake

Blue silence beyond the clouds
erases the jet's trail, a hawk glides
over the lake, and the doe raises her head.

Two dragonflies hang in the air, then zigzag
through the reeds in a game of pursuit, unaware
of the trout watching from its watery bed.

The oak's shadow stretches over
the wrinkled surface to disappear
in clouds of green shimmers.

Wobbling on three legs, the fawn stands
to scratch an offending flea; his ears, too big
for his tiny frame, search for his absent mother.

A study in clumsy grace, he bends his knees
to sink down, hind end last, and blends again
with the forest floor of leaf and twig, light and shadow.

He will remain there, unmoving obedience,
until the moon shines over the water, and the doe
returns to lead him to the meadow to play.

Fish slumber on the muddy lake-bottom, fireflies rest
in the reeds. From his perch on the oak tree,
the hawk cocks his head toward the sky.

When the plane glides through the night to pass
through a cloud with a tremor, the sleeping
passenger turns his head and sighs.

Montana

The mountains remember to watch over this hill
where my parents lie. Over the years,
three sisters, one brother, and my husband have joined their rest.

Blue-shouldered and white-peaked, the giants look down,
faithful to their task, uncaring in their majesty,
while an eagle screams, then dives to snatch a gopher.

The wind whispers each inhale,
sighs each exhale through the lodgepole pines.
In the meadow below, the creek winds around the hill's base,
so clear you can see trout dart through the water like
errant thoughts.

In the shade of its elderly ancestor, baby sagebrush dares to grow;
from the branches of the dying white pine,
cones drop like a waterfall.
Carried by snowmelt and May rain,

deer droppings, bear scat, and cow manure feed
wildflowers' young roots. Elephant's head, buttercups,
shooting stars paint the moist earth purple and yellow.

In late June when spring's melt gives way to stone-hard earth,
wildflowers wither, parched by the sun. On chiseled granite,
lichens spread to cover my mother's name.

I pick up rocks, gritty with warm dust, to fill the badger's hole
near my husband's grave. A breeze bites my cheek with the prickle
of snow from mountains that never sleep.

Walking Sleep

Dust, once the mulch of succulent leaves,
lies undisturbed along the pathway,
silently receiving the print
of bear, bird, and mouse.

You stumble onto their tracks, feet scuffing
the powder to erase the footprint
of a passing deer. In your somnolence
you are less aware than the dust itself,
less aware than the stag that watches
from the shadows, silent majesty.

The din of your passage causes him
to erupt in a crash of smashing dry leaves,
and you are shocked awake,
with dust on your shoes.

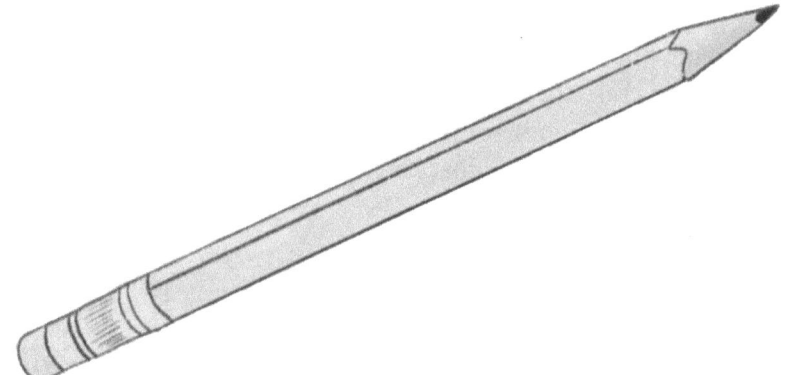

Seasoned with Humor

A Riddle

Clue Number One:
He is known far and wide
as an eavesdropper, but does not
deserve the reputation.
Lacking curiosity, he turns a deaf ear
on private conversation
and looks the other way
from ugly confrontation.

Clue Number Two:
He is also reputed to be irresponsible,
causing widespread disturbance—
he's a terrible nuisance. Yet little
is it considered that he does his job quickly,
rain or shine, even when sickly.

Clue Number Three:
And worst of all, people say
he's a detriment to healing salves.
But it is not his fault that in fulfilling his duty
he sometimes falls victim to substances
sticky and lacking in beauty.

Who is he, you ask, and how is he known?
If by this verse that has not yet been shown,
seek, if you must, the answers below.
But even there, to your woe, as this poet is perverse,
the solution is expressed, alas, in reverse.

llawehtnoylfa :eno
ylfdaga :owt
tnemtnioehtniylfa :eerht

When PG&E Cuts Our Power

we suffer from that new malady called
Smartphone Deprivation Syndrome—SPDS—
an incurable disease which threatens our population
with Total Cyber Paralysis—TCP. Symptoms include
twitching thumbs, glazed eyes, and uncontrollable urges to yawn.

As the days go by without remission, our condition
deteriorates and we must get help before
our prognosis becomes hopeless. We stagger
onto the streets and seek out other sufferers
to engage in face-to-face conversation therapy.

This ominous practice, it is said, will destroy
communication as we know it and will throw us back
to the days when social interaction was the norm,
when we would talk with our neighbor over the fence,
or meet our friend for coffee and conversation.

To ensure we will not revert to such antiquated
behavior, Peegee-n-ee provides us with a tent
to recharge our portable electronics.
We will never (be able to)* thank these pillars of the community
for their kindhearted thoughtfulness in our time of need.

> * include this parenthetical phrase
> (if you are under PG&E's gaze
> as, heaven forbid, they may forego
> repairing your street's transformer
> that was deficient decades ago.)

Montana Recipes

I was raised on a diet of common sense
gently seasoned with humor.
When times were hard we made do
with stewed buttonholes and fried rabbit tracks,
recipes concocted during the Great Depression
and carefully passed from father to son.

We knew some mean old coots in those days;
one was said to be tough as a boiled owl.
That recipe went back to the times
when those hills yonder were already old
and it was passed from mother to daughter.

Zhuzh

I just learned that zhuzh up
means to spruce up, to bring up to date,
and yank now means to give a quick hug.
Maybe I'm so old-fashioned I should be zhuzhed up
so as not be an anachronism, or the day will come, alas,
when I won't understand a single thing people say.

You will have to excuse me to strangers, explain to them
that I don't speak English. I'll totter to my grave, mumbling
incomprehensible words in olde englishe, like mellifluous
superabundant beatification, or conversely, unctuous
naysayer ignoramus. Perhaps in the afterlife there are no words
unless they are poems or the lyrics of songs.

No Batteries Required

I write in pencil, the original computer
of pine wood, graphite, and rubber,
instead of metal, plastic,
and that mysterious something called circuitry.
This small computational device
is simple and just:
one end for **ENTER**, the other for **DELETE**,
no batteries required.

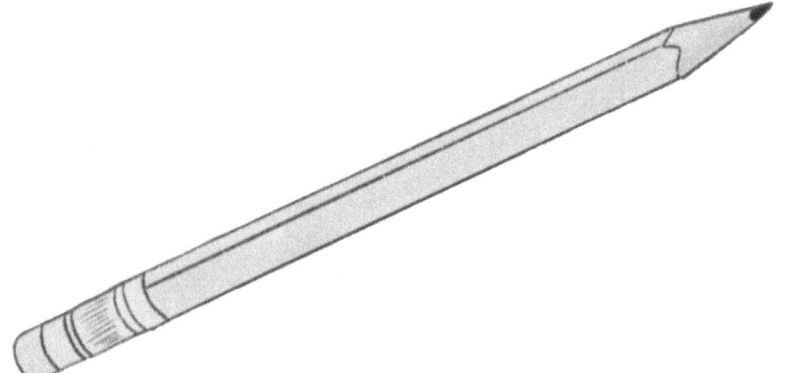

Ellen Dooling Reynard spent her childhood on a cattle ranch in Jackson, Montana. Raised on myths and fairy tales, the sense of wonder has never left her. A one-time editor of *Parabola Magazine*, her poetry has been published by *Lighten Up On Line, Current Magazine, Persimmon, Silver Blade*, and *The Muddy River Poetry Review*. She is now retired and has recently relocated to Clarksville, Maryland, where she will continue to write fiction and poetry. Ellen is currently working on a series of ekphrastic poems based on the work of her late husband, Paul Reynard (1927–2005). You can find her on Facebook.

Thank you for supporting independent publishing.

Yellow Arrow Publishing is a nonprofit supporting writers that identify as women. Visit YellowArrowPublishing.com for information on our publications, workshops, and writing opportunities.

www.ingramcontent.com/pod-product-compliance
Lightning Source LLC
Chambersburg PA
CBHW021130080526
44587CB00012B/1226